OLiVeR

The True Story of a Pup
with 3 Legs and a Heart of Gold

This book is dedicated to Susanna, to Mutts in Need Dog Rescue, to the Topp Family, and of course, to Oliver.

Once upon a time, in the cold winter snow, roamed a small scruffy pup whose tale you should know.

He would roam the streets, and for food
he would beg, Because this pup, you see,
was born missing one leg.

The people in town had this silly
view that a dog must be perfect to
have a heart that was true.

Oliver was no purebred,
he had no fancy papers,
So away he was sent by his
cruel human neighbors.

But one day a woman with a kind look in her eye saw poor Oliver as she was passing by.

"I can tell you need help," the nice lady said, as she gave the sweet stray a scratch on the head.

She called some dog rescuers who thought of a plan to buy Ollie a ticket to a faraway land.

It wasn't long until Oliver's
first adventure had begun.

And when he arrived, he felt
the California sun!

The pup was given some toys,
a bath and a ball.

Maybe this place wasn't bad
after all!

The pooch was taken to a vet who helped his three legs grow stronger.

As the days passed, he learned to run faster and longer.

The rescuers taught him that humans could be gentle and kind, and that he'd never again be left behind.

At the rescue Oliver
made friend after friend,
but he longed for a family
to love and defend.

Sometimes at night he would lie awake and his sweet, loving heart would begin to ache.

He'd glance at his legs and he'd see only three. And he'd think with great sadness, "why would anyone want me?"

One day, as if Oliver's wish had been understood, a mom and daughter came to visit, and he could tell they were good. Oliver's heart raced and nearly skipped a beat as the humans picked the dogs they wanted to meet.

Oliver just couldn't stand it,
he could no longer wait...
so he bolted across the yard and
pushed right through the gate!

He ran to the mother, who jumped with surprise,
"Oh, please choose me," he thought, as he looked
in her eyes.

Ollie wagged his tail and he sat up straight,
and then it came, the moment of fate.

The mother and daughter looked down below.

When they saw only three legs, they whispered,
"Oh..."

His gleaming brown eyes were so hopeful and true,
and his heart was so pure all the way through.
"This dog is perfect in his own special way,
and I think that we'd like to adopt him today."

Oliver could hardly believe his ears.
His tail hadn't wagged faster in all of his years!

He said goodbye to the rescuers
who gave him a chance
And leapt into the car in a big,
happy dance.

He was on his way now to a brand new place
and you should have seen the size of the smile
on his face!

As the weeks passed Oliver's new family discovered that the bright young pup had completely recovered. He was smart, he was strong, and everyone agreed...

no dog at the park
could match his
speed!

A dog doesn't need papers to deserve a human's loving touch and a dog's breed or color really doesn't matter much.

Whether young or old,
whether three legs or four,
a dog's heart of gold is what
we ought to adore.

And as Oliver settled down in the place he belonged,
his heart no longer ached, his mind no longer longed.
"My story isn't ending," Ollie thought with a grin,
"My wonderful life is just about to begin!"

Did you know that Oliver's story is true?

Oliver was born as a stray puppy in Armenia. When a dog rescuer found Oliver and sent him to the United States, he was adopted by the Topp family, who love him with all of their hearts. Oliver doesn't let the fact that he has three legs stop him, and he can be found running, wrestling and playing at the beach or the dog park just about any day of the week. There is no need to feel sorry for Oliver- he gets around just fine and always has a big, goofy smile on his face. Some people even say he's the fastest dog around!

To make a donation or learn more about the wonderful dog rescue group that saved Oliver's life, please visit muttsinneed.org. Oliver and all his rescued pals hope that you will consider adopting your next furry friend from an animal shelter or rescue group!

Visit *luckylambbooks.com*
to order a new copy of this book today!
A portion of proceeds from each book sold is
donated to help rescued dogs like Oliver find their
forever homes.

Lucky Lamb Books

CPSIA information can be obtained
at www.ICGtesting.com
Printed in the USA
BVHW021247271019
562118BV00002B/2/P